Entry Level Accounting Interview Guide
by Shahida J

- All Copyrights Reserved© 2024

-
- **Importance of acing the interview for an entry-level accounting job:** Understand how a strong performance in your interview can kick-start your career in accounting.

- **Overview of the book's contents and how it can help the reader:** This guide offers a detailed and comprehensive compilation of interview questions, ensuring thorough preparation for entry-level accounting interviews. Covering comprehensively all areas an interviewer can ask questions; this book equips you with the insights and strategies needed to succeed and build confidence as you embark on your accounting career journey.

Entry Level Accounting -Interview Guide

Table of Content

Table of Content---3

Introduction---6

Chapter 1: Understanding the Accounting Profession -21

Chapter 2: Preparing for the Interview----------------------33

Chapter 3 Common Interview Questions and Answers-42

Chapter 4: Asking Insightful Question------------------------102

Chapter 5: Following Up After the Interview---------------105

Chapter 6: Additional Tips and Resources-----------------109

- Importance of acing the interview for an entry-level accounting job
- Overview of the book's contents and how it can help the reader

Chapter 1: Understanding the Accounting Profession

- Brief overview of the accounting field and its various roles
- Responsibilities and duties of an entry-level accountant
- Desired skills and qualities for accounting professionals

Chapter 2: Preparing for the Interview

- Researching the company and the role
- Reviewing common interview questions for entry-level accounting positions
- Practicing your responses and body language
- Dressing professionally for the interview

3: Common Interview Questions and Answers

- "Tell me about yourself" and how to craft an effective elevator pitch
- Questions about your education, coursework, and academic achievements
- Behavioral questions and how to use the STAR method to answer them
- Technical accounting questions and how to demonstrate your knowledge
- Questions about your strengths, weaknesses, and areas for improvement
- Questions about your interest in the company and the role

Chapter 4: Asking Insightful Questions

- The importance of asking meaningful questions during the interview
- Examples of good questions to ask about the company, team, and role
- Questions to avoid asking during an interview

Chapter 5: Following Up After the Interview

- Writing a thank-you note and its significance
- Evaluating your performance and identifying areas for improvement
- Handling job offers and negotiations

Chapter 6: Additional Tips and Resources

- Networking and building professional relationships
- Continuing education and professional development opportunities
- Recommended books, websites, and other resources for aspiring accountants

Introduction

Whether they are changing careers later in life or are just out of college, many people find themselves starting a new career in accounting. Even while the change can be exhilarating, it's normal to experience a range of feelings, including excitement, curiosity, and possibly some trepidation about embarking on a new career path.

Success on this journey depends on having the appropriate mindset going into it. Possessing an open and growth-oriented mindset as well as a readiness to change and progress can be quite beneficial. Accept obstacles as chances for both professional and personal development, and face failures head-on with resiliency and resolve. Maintaining an optimistic outlook can not only help you feel more confident, but it will also leave a lasting impression on prospective employers. It will be beneficial to keep a healthy balance between arrogance and humility.

Securing an entry-level accounting job is an exciting first step in a rewarding and lucrative career path. However, the interview process can be daunting, especially for those who are new to the professional world. With numerous qualified candidates vying for the same position, it's crucial to make a strong and lasting impression during the interview.

This comprehensive guide is designed to provide you with the tools and strategies necessary to ace your interview for an entry-level accounting job. Whether you're a recent

Entry Level Accounting -Interview Guide

graduate or a career-changer, this book will equip you with the knowledge and confidence to showcase your skills, expertise, and passion for the accounting profession.

Throughout these pages, you'll find invaluable insights and practical advice to help you prepare for every stage of the interview process. From understanding the accounting profession and its expectations to crafting compelling responses to common interview questions, this book covers it all.

You'll learn how to research the company and the role, practice your responses and body language, and dress professionally for the interview. Additionally, you'll gain insights into answering behavioral and technical accounting questions, as well as strategies for asking insightful questions of your own.

The book also addresses the importance of following up after the interview, including writing a thoughtful thank-you note and evaluating your performance. Furthermore, it provides guidance on handling job offers and negotiations, should you receive them.

Beyond the interview itself, this guide offers additional tips and resources to help you continue your professional development and stay ahead in the competitive accounting field. From networking and building professional relationships to exploring continuing education opportunities, you'll find valuable information to support your long-term career growth.

With a combination of practical advice, real-life examples, and expert insights, this book is your ultimate companion in your pursuit of an entry-level accounting job. Whether you're feeling nervous or confident, this guide will empower you to present your best self and increase your chances of landing your dream job.

Great Attributes that Go Along

Here are 10 great attributes to start a new career with, along with explanations and examples:

1. Enthusiasm and Passion
    - Approach your new career with genuine excitement and a deep interest in the field.
    - Example: An accounting graduate who is thrilled about analyzing financial data and helping businesses make informed decisions.
2. Adaptability and Flexibility
    - Be open to change and willing to adjust to new situations, processes, and environments.
    - Example: A career-changer who embraces the transition from their previous role and is eager to learn the accounting principles and software.
3. Coachability and Willingness to Learn
    - Have a humble attitude and a desire to continuously learn and improve.
    - Example: A new hire who actively seeks feedback from experienced colleagues and applies their guidance to enhance their skills.
4. Strong Work Ethic

- Demonstrate dedication, punctuality, and a commitment to putting in the effort required for success.
- Example: An entry-level accountant who consistently arrives early, meets deadlines, and goes the extra mile on assignments.

5. Attention to Detail
   - Develop a keen eye for accuracy and the ability to catch even the smallest errors or discrepancies.
   - Example: A junior accountant who meticulously reviews financial statements and catches a minor calculation error.

6. Analytical and Critical Thinking Skills
   - Possess the ability to analyze complex data, identify patterns, and solve problems logically.
   - Example: A new accountant who can interpret financial reports and provide insights into improving profitability.

7. Excellent Communication Skills
   - Clearly articulate ideas, actively listen, and effectively collaborate with teams and clients.
   - Example: A recent graduate who can concisely explain accounting concepts to non-financial colleagues during presentations.

8. Time Management and Organizational Skills
   - Prioritize tasks, manage deadlines, and maintain an organized workspace and workflow.
   - Example: An entry-level accountant who creates a system to track multiple client engagements and meet all filing deadlines.

9. Professionalism and Integrity
    - Consistently conduct yourself with ethical standards, confidentiality, and a commitment to honesty.
    - Example: A career-changer who handles sensitive financial information with discretion and adheres to industry regulations.

10. Continuous Improvement and Growth Mindset
    - Embrace challenges as opportunities for growth and actively seek ways to enhance your knowledge and skillset.
    - Example: A new accountant who enrolls in professional development courses and seeks opportunities to expand their expertise.

You'll be more prepared to handle the chances and difficulties that come with launching a new accounting job if you work on developing these qualities. Recall that success requires not only technical expertise but also the appropriate attitude, work habits, and personal traits.

Networking is Essential

Building a network is crucial for professional advancement, especially when launching a new accounting career. Establishing a robust professional network can yield a multitude of advantages and prospects. The following list of top networking concepts and five justifications for networking is helpful:

1. Access to Job Opportunities Networking can open doors to potential job openings and career advancement. Many job openings are not advertised publicly, and personal connections can give you an inside track. Networking allows you to learn about unadvertised positions and get referrals from your contacts. Best Networking Idea: Attend industry events, conferences, or meetups related to accounting and finance. Introduce yourself to professionals in the field and express your interest in potential job opportunities.

2. Acquiring Knowledge and Guidance Through networking, you can get in touch with seasoned experts who can provide insightful commentary, wise counsel, and mentoring. They can offer advice on careers, share their experiences, and guide you over obstacles in the accounting industry. Top Networking Suggestion: Make contact with former students from your college or university who are employed by accounting firms or other businesses that interest you. To get insights and understand more about their professional path, ask for an informational interview.

3. Building Relationships and Expanding Your Circle Networking allows you to build relationships with

professionals in your industry. These connections can lead to future collaborations, referrals, or even friendships that can benefit your personal and professional growth. Best Networking Idea: Join professional organizations or associations related to accounting, such as the American Institute of CPAs (AICPA) or local chapters. Attend their events and actively participate in discussions or volunteer opportunities to meet new people.

4. Remaining Current with Sector Trends You can stay up to date on the newest developments in accounting, including innovative technology, best practices, and trends, via networking. Your network can offer insightful information on modifications to laws, software, or business advancements. The best way to network is to follow well-known accounting companies, individuals, and publications on social media sites like Twitter and LinkedIn. Participate in dialogues, exchange content, and add to topics to expand your network and online profile.

5. Building Confidence and Communication Skills Networking allows you to practice and improve your communication skills, which are essential in the accounting profession. By regularly engaging with professionals, you'll gain confidence in introducing yourself, pitching your skills, and articulating your thoughts clearly. Best Networking Idea: Volunteer to speak at local events,

workshops, or student organizations. Sharing your knowledge and experiences can help you build confidence in public speaking and networking with others in the accounting field.

Remember, networking is not just about collecting business cards or attending events. It's about building genuine connections, offering value to others, and actively nurturing your professional relationships over time.

Counter the Opposition Within

It may be an exciting and difficult trip to launch a new career, and it's normal to have setbacks along the road. But it's critical to identify these challenges and devise plans of action to get over them. Here are seven systematic strategies for fending off discouragement when it tries to pursue you:

1. Embrace a Growth Mindset
    - Discouragement often stems from a fixed mindset, where setbacks are perceived as failures.
    - Counter-attack: Adopt a growth mindset, viewing challenges as opportunities for learning and improvement.
    - Example: Instead of feeling discouraged after a difficult interview, reflect on the areas you can improve and seek feedback for growth.

2. Celebrate Small Wins
    - Discouragement can creep in when you focus solely on the end goal, overlooking the progress you've made.
    - Counter-attack: Recognize and celebrate small victories along the way to maintain motivation and momentum.
    - Example: Treat yourself to a small reward after successfully networking with professionals in your desired field.
3. Seek Support and Mentorship
    - Discouragement can feel isolating, making it easy to lose perspective and confidence.
    - Counter-attack: Build a supportive network of mentors, peers, or friends who can offer encouragement and guidance.
    - Example: Join a professional association or find a mentor who can share their experiences and provide advice during challenging times.
4. Practice Self-Care
    - Discouragement can be exacerbated by burnout, stress, and neglecting your well-being.
    - Counter-attack: Prioritize self-care activities that rejuvenate your mind, body, and spirit.
    - Example: Maintain a healthy work-life balance by engaging in exercise, hobbies, or spending quality time with loved ones.
5. Reframe Setbacks
    - Discouragement often stems from perceiving setbacks as failures rather than learning opportunities.

- Counter-attack: Reframe setbacks as chances to identify areas for improvement and adapt your approach.
- Example: If you're not selected for a job, reflect on the feedback received and use it to enhance your interview skills for future opportunities.

6. Visualize Success
   - Discouragement can make it challenging to maintain a positive outlook and envision achieving your goals.
   - Counter-attack: Engage in visualization exercises, imagining yourself succeeding and overcoming obstacles.
   - Example: Create a vision board or write affirmations to remind yourself of your aspirations and the progress you've made

7. Seek Professional Support
   - In some cases, discouragement can be deeply rooted and require additional support.
   - Counter-attack: Consider seeking guidance from a career coach, therapist, or counselor who can provide professional assistance.
   - Example: Work with a career coach to develop strategies for overcoming self-doubt and building confidence during your job search.

Remember, discouragement is a natural part of any journey, but it's how you respond that determines your ultimate success. By adopting these counter-attack strategies, you can cultivate resilience, maintain motivation, and continue progressing towards your career goals in accounting.

Entry Level Accounting -Interview Guide

Stick to the Plan

Navigating the ups and downs of a new professional path requires sticking to your plan and accepting that there will be better moments to think about other occupations. The following seven themes highlight the need of sticking to the plan while being flexible enough to make possible detours:

1. Patience and Perseverance
    - Success in a new career rarely happens overnight; it requires consistent effort and a long-term mindset.
    - Sticking to your plan allows you to develop the necessary skills, experience, and expertise over time.
    - Example: Resist the urge to switch careers after a few months of challenges, as mastering accounting principles and practices takes time and dedication.
2. Comprehensive Evaluation
    - Before considering alternate careers, conduct a thorough evaluation of your current situation and progress.
    - Identify specific areas of struggle and explore strategies to overcome them before making drastic changes.
    - Example: If you're facing difficulties with technical accounting concepts, seek additional training or mentorship rather than abandoning the field altogether.
3. Adaptability and Flexibility

- While sticking to your plan is important, maintain an open mind and be willing to adapt your approach as circumstances change.
- Embrace opportunities for growth and learning, even if they deviate slightly from your initial plan.
- Example: If a promising opportunity arises in a related field, such as financial analysis or auditing, consider exploring it while still leveraging your accounting knowledge.

4. Short-term vs. Long-term Goals
    - Differentiate between short-term challenges and long-term career aspirations.
    - Temporary setbacks or frustrations should not overshadow your overall goals and motivations.
    - Example: A difficult project or demanding client may be disheartening in the moment, but it can also provide valuable experience for future growth in the accounting field.

5. Reassess Periodically
    - While sticking to your plan is crucial, it's also important to periodically reassess your goals and priorities.

Entry Level Accounting -Interview Guide

- o As you gain more experience and exposure, your interests or aspirations may evolve.
- o Example: After working in public accounting for a few years, you may realize that your true passion lies in corporate finance or forensic accounting, prompting a thoughtful career transition

.

6. Seek Advice and Mentorship
    - o Consult with experienced professionals or mentors for guidance on navigating career challenges and potential pivots.
    - o Their insights and perspectives can help you make informed decisions about sticking to your plan or exploring alternate paths.
    - o Example: Discuss your concerns and aspirations with a seasoned accountant who can provide objective advice on whether it's best to persist or consider a change.
7. Embrace Lifelong Learning
8.
    - o Recognize that career paths are rarely linear, and continue to invest in your personal and professional development.
    - o Continuously acquiring new skills and knowledge can open doors to alternate careers or advanced roles within your field.
    - o Example: Pursue certifications, attend industry events, or enroll in continuing

education courses to expand your expertise and increase your career flexibility.

By sticking to your plan while remaining open to potential pivots, you can navigate the challenges of a new career with resilience and adaptability. Remember, the journey may not always be linear, but perseverance, self-reflection, and a willingness to learn can ultimately lead you to a fulfilling and rewarding career path.

Are you ready to embark on this exciting journey? Let's get started

Chapter 1: Understanding the Accounting Profession for the book on interview help for an entry-level accounting job:

Understanding the Accounting Profession

Before embarking on your journey to secure an entry-level accounting job, it's essential to have a solid understanding of the accounting profession itself. This chapter will provide an overview of the field, its various roles and responsibilities, and the desired skills and qualities for successful accounting professionals.

Management Accounting vs. Financial Accounting

Within the broad field of accounting, there are two main branches that serve distinct purposes: management accounting and financial accounting. While both involve the analysis and reporting of financial data, they differ in their primary objectives, stakeholders, and methodologies.

Management Accounting Management accounting is focused on providing financial information and analysis to internal stakeholders, such as managers, executives, and decision-makers within an organization. Its primary goal is to assist in strategic planning, budgeting, cost management, and performance evaluation.

Key aspects of cost accounting include:

1. Cost Accounting: Analyzing and controlling costs related to products, services, and operational processes, enabling informed decision-making and cost optimization.
2. Budgeting and Forecasting: Preparing budgets and financial forecasts to allocate resources effectively and monitor actual performance against projected targets.
3. Performance Measurement: Developing and tracking key performance indicators (KPIs) to assess the efficiency and profitability of various business units, products, or initiatives.
4. Strategic Planning and Decision Analysis: Providing financial analysis and data-driven insights to support strategic decision-making, such as pricing strategies, capital investments, and resource allocation.

Management accountants work closely with operational teams and executives, acting as strategic business partners and advisors to drive informed decision-making and continuous improvement within the organization.

Financial Accounting Financial accounting, on the other hand, focuses on the preparation and reporting of financial statements and information for external stakeholders, such as investors, creditors, regulatory bodies, and the general public. Its primary objective is to provide a transparent and standardized representation of an organization's financial performance and position.

Entry Level Accounting - Interview Guide

Key aspects of financial accounting include:

1. Financial Statement Preparation: Developing and presenting financial statements, including the balance sheet, income statement, statement of cash flows, and accompanying notes, in accordance with generally accepted accounting principles (GAAP) or international financial reporting standards (IFRS).
2. External Reporting and Compliance: Ensuring that financial reporting adheres to relevant laws, regulations, and accounting standards, enabling stakeholders to make informed decisions based on reliable and accurate information.
3. Auditing: Facilitating the independent verification of financial statements and internal controls by external auditors to ensure accuracy and compliance.
4. Tax Reporting: Preparing tax returns and ensuring compliance with applicable tax laws and regulations.

Here are the key aspects of management accounting and financial accounting:

Management Accounting:

Cost Accounting:

- Analyze and allocate costs to products, services, and processes for better cost control.
- Identify areas for cost optimization and process improvements.

- Provide insights into pricing strategies and profitability analysis.

Budgeting and Forecasting:

- Prepare detailed budgets aligning with organizational goals and strategies.
- Forecast future revenues, expenses, and cash flows for effective resource planning.
- Monitor actual performance against budgeted targets and make necessary adjustments.

Performance Measurement:

- Develop and track key performance indicators (KPIs) across various business units.
- Assess operational efficiency, productivity, and profitability using financial and non-financial metrics.
- Identify areas for improvement and implement corrective actions.

Strategic Planning and Decision Analysis:

- Conduct financial modeling and scenario analysis for strategic decision-making.
- Evaluate potential investments, mergers, acquisitions, or expansion opportunities.
- Provide data-driven insights to support long-term business strategies and resource allocation.

Financial Accounting:

Financial Statement Preparation:

Entry Level Accounting - Interview Guide

- Prepare accurate and compliant financial statements according to GAAP or IFRS.
- Ensure proper recording, classification, and reporting of financial transactions.
- Provide clear and transparent disclosure of an organization's financial position and performance.

External Reporting and Compliance:

- Adhere to relevant laws, regulations, and accounting standards in financial reporting.
- Maintain documentation and support for financial statements and disclosures.
- Communicate financial information to external stakeholders, such as investors and regulators.

Auditing:

- Coordinate with external auditors to facilitate the audit process.
- Provide necessary documentation and support for financial statement audits.
- Ensure internal controls and processes are in place for accurate financial reporting.

Tax Reporting:

- Prepare and file tax returns in compliance with applicable tax laws and regulations.
- Analyze tax implications of business transactions and strategies.
- Implement tax planning strategies to minimize tax liabilities while adhering to regulations.

Shahida J.

These lines provide a brief overview of the key responsibilities and focus areas within management accounting and financial accounting, highlighting their distinct yet complementary roles in supporting organizational decision-making and maintaining financial transparency and compliance.

Financial accountants work closely with auditors, regulatory bodies, and stakeholders to maintain transparency, integrity, and compliance in financial reporting.

While management accounting and financial accounting serve different purposes, they are interconnected and complementary within an organization. Effective collaboration and communication between management accountants and financial accountants are crucial for ensuring accurate and comprehensive financial management and decision-making.

Entry Level Accounting - Interview Guide

Understanding the distinctions between these two branches of accounting will better prepare you for potential interview questions and discussions related to your desired role and responsibilities within the accounting profession.

The Accounting Field: A Brief Overview Accounting is often referred to as the "language of business." It involves the systematic recording, analyzing, and reporting of financial transactions and information for individuals, businesses, and organizations. At its core, accounting enables stakeholders to make informed decisions based on accurate and transparent financial data.

Roles and Responsibilities in Accounting The accounting profession encompasses a diverse range of roles and responsibilities, each playing a crucial part in ensuring financial integrity and compliance. Here are some of the key areas within the field:

1. Public Accounting
    - Public accountants work for accounting firms and provide services such as auditing, tax preparation, and consulting to clients ranging from individuals to large corporations.
    - Roles in public accounting include staff accountants, audit associates, tax associates, and consultants.

2. Corporate Accounting
    - Corporate accountants are employed by companies and organizations to manage internal financial operations, such as bookkeeping, financial reporting, budgeting, and compliance with regulations.
    - Roles in corporate accounting include staff accountants, accounts payable/receivable clerks, financial analysts, and controllers.

3. Governmental and Non-Profit Accounting
    - Governmental and non-profit accountants work for public sector organizations, such as government agencies, schools, hospitals, and charities.
    - Their responsibilities include managing and reporting financial information, ensuring compliance with regulations, and overseeing budgets and funding.

4. Forensic Accounting
    - Forensic accountants investigate and analyze financial data to detect and prevent fraud, embezzlement, and other financial crimes.
    - They may work for law enforcement agencies, accounting firms, or as independent consultants.

Desired Skills and Qualities To succeed in the accounting profession, individuals must possess a combination of technical skills, analytical abilities, and personal qualities. Some of the key skills and qualities sought after in accounting professionals include:

Entry Level Accounting -Interview Guide

Skills that Make you a Strong Candidate

Here's a suggested methodology to adopt for developing and demonstrating the desired skills and qualities for successful accounting professionals:

1. Strong numerical and analytical skills:
    - Practice solving complex numerical problems and financial calculations regularly.
    - Develop proficiency in using spreadsheets, databases, and analytical tools.
    - Enroll in courses or workshops focused on quantitative analysis and data interpretation.
    - Seek opportunities to analyze financial data and identify patterns or trends.
2. Attention to detail and accuracy:
    - Implement a systematic approach to reviewing and double-checking your work.
    - Develop checklists or quality control processes to minimize errors.
    - Practice proofreading and verifying calculations, entries, and reports meticulously.
    - Cultivate a mindset of precision and accuracy in all tasks.
3. Problem-solving and critical thinking abilities:
    - Analyze case studies or real-world scenarios to identify problems and propose solutions.
    - Engage in discussions or simulations that require critical thinking and decision-making.

- Seek feedback from experienced professionals on your problem-solving approach.
- Continuously challenge assumptions and consider alternative perspectives.

4. Proficiency in accounting software and technology:
    - Familiarize yourself with industry-standard accounting software and tools.
    - Attend training sessions or enroll in courses to enhance your software skills.
    - Stay up-to-date with technological advancements in the accounting field.
    - Explore opportunities to apply technology in improving accounting processes.

5. Excellent communication and interpersonal skills:
    - Practice active listening and effective communication in professional settings.
    - Seek opportunities to present information or lead discussions to improve public speaking skills.
    - Develop strong written communication skills by practicing report writing and documentation.
    - Build interpersonal skills by participating in team projects or group activities

6. Time management and organizational skills:
    - Utilize calendars, task lists, and project management tools to prioritize and track responsibilities.

- o Develop systems and processes to streamline workflows and improve efficiency.
- o Practice time-boxing techniques to allocate focused time for important tasks.
- o Maintain organized workspaces and digital filing systems for easy retrieval of information.

7. Ethical integrity and commitment to confidentiality:
    - o Familiarize yourself with professional codes of conduct and ethical guidelines.
    - o Participate in ethics training or workshops to reinforce ethical principles.
    - o Develop a deep understanding of confidentiality requirements and data protection regulations.
    - o Cultivate a mindset of trust, honesty, and accountability in all professional interactions.

8. Continuous learning and professional development:
    - o Stay informed about industry trends, regulatory changes, and best practices.
    - o Attend professional conferences, seminars, or webinars to expand your knowledge.
    - o Pursue additional certifications or educational opportunities relevant to your career goals.

- Seek mentorship or join professional associations to learn from experienced professionals.

By adopting a proactive and structured approach to developing these essential skills and qualities, you can position yourself as a well-rounded and competitive candidate for entry-level accounting roles. Remember, continuous improvement and a commitment to lifelong learning are key to long-term success in the accounting profession.

As you prepare for your entry-level accounting job interviews, understanding the diverse nature of the accounting profession, its various roles and responsibilities, and the essential skills and qualities required will help you present yourself as a well-informed and motivated candidate.

In the following chapters, we will delve deeper into strategies for effectively showcasing your knowledge, skills, and passion for the accounting field during the interview process

Entry Level Accounting -Interview Guide

Chapter 2: Preparing for the Interview

Thorough preparation is essential to make a strong and lasting impression during an interview for an entry-level accounting position. This chapter will guide you through the crucial steps of researching the company and the role, reviewing common interview questions, practicing your responses and body language, and dressing professionally for the interview.

Researching the Company and the Role

Before attending an interview, it's imperative to gain a comprehensive understanding of the company and the specific role you're applying for. This research will not only demonstrate your genuine interest and commitment but also equip you with valuable insights to tailor your responses and ask informed questions.

1. Company Background and Culture:
    - Study the company's website, mission statement, values, and history.
    - Explore the company's products, services, and target market.
    - Research recent news, press releases, or industry publications about the company.
    - Understand the company's culture, work environment, and employee reviews (if available).

2. Industry Landscape and Competitors:
   - Familiarize yourself with the industry trends, challenges, and opportunities.
   - Identify the company's major competitors and their market positioning.
   - Stay updated on relevant regulations, technological advancements, or economic factors impacting the industry.
3. Role and Responsibilities:
   - Carefully review the job description and requirements for the entry-level accounting position.
   - Understand the specific duties, tasks, and skills required for the role.
   - Identify how your qualifications and experiences align with the job responsibilities.

Reviewing Common Interview Questions for Entry-Level Accounting Positions

Anticipating and preparing for common interview questions can help you formulate thoughtful and compelling responses. Here are some typical questions you may encounter:

1. "Tell me about yourself."
   - This is an opportunity to provide a concise overview of your background, education, and relevant experiences.
   - Highlight your strengths, accomplishments, and passion for the accounting field

Entry Level Accounting -Interview Guide

2. Questions about your education and coursework:
    - Be prepared to discuss your academic achievements, relevant courses, and any accounting-related projects or internships.
    - Explain how your education has prepared you for an entry-level accounting role.
3. Behavioral questions (e.g., "Describe a time when..."):
    - These questions aim to assess your problem-solving abilities, teamwork skills, and how you handle challenging situations.
    - Use the STAR (Situation, Task, Action, Result) method to structure your responses.
4. Technical accounting questions: (We will come to this later in the book to discuss in detail)
    - Expect questions that test your knowledge of accounting principles, financial statements, and industry-specific concepts.
    - Review key accounting concepts, terminologies, and be prepared to demonstrate your technical proficiency.
5. Questions about your strengths, weaknesses, and areas for improvement:
    - Provide honest and thoughtful responses, highlighting your self-awareness and commitment to continuous growth.
    - Frame your weaknesses as areas for improvement and explain how you're actively working on them.
6. Questions about your interest in the company and the role:

- Demonstrate your enthusiasm and genuine interest in the company and the position.
- Relate your skills, experiences, and goals to the company's mission and the role's responsibilities.

Practicing Your Responses and Body Language

After reviewing common interview questions and formulating your responses, it's crucial to practice delivering them effectively. Consider the following strategies:

1. Mock Interviews:
     - Conduct practice interviews with friends, family members, or career counselors.
     - Seek feedback on your responses, body language, and overall demeanor.
     - Refine your responses based on the feedback received.
2. Recording Yourself:
     - Record yourself answering interview questions and watch the playback.
     - Evaluate your tone, pace, and nonverbal cues, and make necessary adjustments.
3. Body Language and Nonverbal Communication:
     - Maintain good posture, make eye contact, and avoid fidgeting or nervous gestures.
     - Practice a firm handshake and a confident, friendly demeanor.
4. Active Listening:

Entry Level Accounting -Interview Guide

- During the interview, listen attentively to the interviewer's questions and respond directly.
- Avoid interrupting or appearing distracted.

Shahida J.
Dressing Professionally for the Interview

Your appearance and attire can significantly impact the first impression you make on the interviewer. Here are some guidelines for dressing professionally:

1. Business Professional Attire:
    - For men: A well-fitted suit (preferably in a conservative color like navy or charcoal), a long-sleeved dress shirt, a tie, and dress shoes.
    - For women: A tailored suit, a blouse or dress shirt, a knee-length skirt or dress pants, and closed-toe dress shoes with a moderate heel.
2. Grooming and Accessories:
    - Maintain a neat and well-groomed appearance, including hair, nails, and minimal makeup (if applicable).
    - Avoid excessive jewelry or strong fragrances.
    - Carry a professional-looking portfolio or briefcase to hold copies of your resume and any necessary documents.
3. Confidence and Comfort:
    - Choose an outfit that fits well and makes you feel confident and comfortable.
    - Ensure your clothing is clean, pressed, and in good condition.

By thoroughly preparing for the interview, practicing your responses, and presenting a professional appearance, you'll increase your chances of making a positive and lasting impression on the interviewer.

Entry Level Accounting - Interview Guide

In the next chapter, we'll delve into common interview questions and strategies for crafting compelling responses that showcase your qualifications, knowledge, and passion for the accounting profession.

What Sets You Apart from Other Candidates

Here are 10 guidelines on what sets you apart from other candidates,

Unique Experiences and Accomplishments:

- Highlight any distinctive experiences, projects, or achievements that demonstrate your skills and potential.
- Example: "During my internship at [Company X], I had the opportunity to work on a complex financial analysis project. (Distinctive Experience) I was tasked with analyzing three years' worth of financial data to identify cost-saving opportunities. (Project) Through my attention to detail and analytical skills, I was able to uncover potential savings of over $100,000 in operational expenses, which I presented to the management team." (Achievement Demonstrating Skills and Potential)

Passion and Enthusiasm:

- Convey your genuine passion for the accounting field and enthusiasm for the role.
- Example: "Ever since I took my first accounting course in college, I was captivated by the intricate world of financial reporting and analysis. (Passion) This passion is what motivated me to pursue a career in accounting, and I'm eager to bring that

enthusiasm to this role. (Enthusiasm for the Role) I find the process of transforming raw data into insightful information that drives business decisions truly fascinating." (Genuine Passion for the Field)

Continuous Learning and Growth Mindset:

- Emphasize your commitment to continuous learning and professional development.
- Example: "I firmly believe that continuous learning is essential for professional growth, especially in the dynamic field of accounting. (Growth Mindset) Last year, I completed the Certified Management Accountant (CMA) certification program to expand my knowledge and demonstrate my commitment to professional development. (Continuous Learning) I'm currently exploring opportunities to further enhance my skills in data analytics and visualization." (Commitment to Professional Development)

Strong Work Ethic and Dedication:

- Demonstrate your strong work ethic, dedication, and willingness to go above and beyond.
- Example: "During my final semester, I juggled a full course load, a part-time accounting internship, and my role as the treasurer for the university's finance club. (Challenging Situation) Despite the demanding schedule, I excelled in all my responsibilities by meticulously managing my time and prioritizing tasks. (Strong Work Ethic) I even

volunteered to take on additional projects at my internship, demonstrating my dedication and willingness to go above and beyond." (Going Above and Beyond)

Adaptability and Problem-Solving Skills:

- Showcase your ability to adapt to changing circumstances and solve complex problems.
- Example: "In my previous role as a student accounting assistant, I encountered a situation where our financial reporting software experienced a glitch, causing delays in generating monthly reports. (Changing Circumstance) I quickly adapted by developing a temporary workaround using spreadsheets and data extraction tools. (Adaptability) This allowed us to meet the reporting deadline while the IT team resolved the software issue, showcasing my problem-solving skills." (Solving Complex Problems)

By effectively highlighting these unique qualities and experiences, you can differentiate yourself from other candidates and demonstrate why you are the ideal choice for the entry-level accounting position. Remember to provide specific examples and tailor your responses to the company's values and the role's requirements.

Chapter 3 Common Interview Questions and Answers

Introduction:

Interviews are nerve-wracking experiences for many, but with preparation and practice, you can navigate them with confidence. This chapter will focus on some of the most common interview questions you might encounter and provide tips on how to craft effective answers.

1. "Tell me about yourself" and how to craft an effective elevator pitch:

When an interviewer asks, "Tell me about yourself," they're not looking for your life story. They want a brief summary of your professional background and relevant experiences. Craft an elevator pitch that highlights your skills, experiences, and accomplishments in a concise and engaging manner. Focus on aspects of your background that are most relevant to the job you're applying for.

Example: "I'm a detail-oriented accountant with five years of experience in financial analysis and reporting. In my previous role at XYZ Company, I implemented a new accounting software that streamlined our processes and reduced errors by 20%. I'm excited about the opportunity to bring my expertise to your team and contribute to the continued success of your organization."

Entry Level Accounting -Interview Guide

2. Questions about your education, coursework, and academic achievements:

Be prepared to discuss your educational background, including any relevant coursework or academic achievements. Highlight any honors, awards, or extracurricular activities that demonstrate your dedication and commitment to your field.

Example: "I graduated with a degree in Accounting from ABC University, where I maintained a GPA of 3.8. During my studies, I participated in internships at two different accounting firms, where I gained hands-on experience in financial analysis and auditing. I was also awarded the Outstanding Accounting Student of the Year award for my academic achievements and leadership qualities."

3. Behavioral questions and how to use the STAR method to answer them:

Behavioral questions are designed to assess your past behavior and how you might handle similar situations in the future. Use the STAR method (Situation, Task, Action, Result) to structure your answers:

- Situation: Describe the context or background of the situation.
- Task: Explain the specific task or challenge you were faced with.
- Action: Detail the actions you took to address the challenge.

- Result: Summarize the outcome of your actions and any lessons learned.

Example: Question: "Tell me about a time when you had to work under pressure to meet a deadline." Answer using the STAR method:

- Situation: "In my previous role, we had a tight deadline to complete the year-end financial report."
- Task: "My task was to gather data from multiple departments and reconcile discrepancies to ensure accuracy."
- Action: "I prioritized tasks, delegated responsibilities, and communicated regularly with team members to ensure we stayed on track."
- Result: "As a result of our efforts, we completed the report ahead of schedule, earning praise from senior management for our efficiency and accuracy."

4. Technical accounting questions and how to demonstrate your knowledge:

Prepare for technical accounting questions related to your field of expertise. Demonstrate your knowledge and problem-solving skills by providing clear and concise answers. If you're unsure about a question, don't be afraid to ask for clarification or take a moment to gather your thoughts before responding.

Entry Level Accounting -Interview Guide

20 Technical questions with answers

5. **Difference between accrual accounting and cash accounting:**

    - Accrual accounting records transactions when they occur, regardless of when cash is exchanged, providing a more accurate picture of a company's financial health.
    - Cash accounting records transactions only when cash is exchanged, reflecting actual cash inflows and outflows.
    - Accrual accounting follows the matching principle, matching revenues with expenses in the period they are incurred.
    - Cash accounting is simpler and more straightforward but may not provide an accurate representation of a company's financial position.
    - Accrual accounting is required for most businesses for financial reporting purposes.

6. **Concept of double-entry accounting:**

    - Double-entry accounting requires every transaction to have equal and opposite entries in at least two different accounts.
    - It ensures that the accounting equation (Assets = Liabilities + Equity) remains balanced

- Each transaction affects at least two accounts, with one account debited and another credited.
- Double-entry accounting provides a systematic way to track and verify the accuracy of financial transactions.
- It is the foundation of modern accounting systems and allows for the creation of accurate financial statements.

7. **Purpose of a trial balance and how it's prepared:**

    - The purpose of a trial balance is to verify that the total debits equal the total credits in the accounting system.
    - It helps identify any errors in recording transactions before preparing financial statements.
    - A trial balance is prepared by listing all accounts and their respective debit or credit balances.
    - Debit balances are listed in one column, and credit balances are listed in another.
    - The total of the debit column should equal the total of the credit column if the books are in balance.

8. **Definition of depreciation and its importance in accounting:**

    - Depreciation is the systematic allocation of the cost of a tangible asset over its useful life.
    - It reflects the gradual reduction in the value of an asset due to wear and tear, obsolescence, or usage.
    - Depreciation is important in accounting because it matches the cost of using the asset with the revenue it generates over time.
    - It helps accurately report the true economic value of assets on the balance sheet.
    - Depreciation expense is recorded on the income statement, reducing the net income and taxable income of a company.

9. **Calculation of gross profit and net profit:**

    - Gross profit is calculated by subtracting the cost of goods sold (COGS) from total revenue.
    - It represents the profit earned from the core business activities before deducting operating expenses.
    - Net profit is calculated by subtracting all expenses, including COGS, operating

expenses, interest, and taxes, from total revenue.

- It represents the profit remaining after all expenses have been deducted.
- Gross profit margin and net profit margin are expressed as percentages and indicate the profitability of a company's operations.

10. - Gross profit margin and net profit margin are expressed as percentages and indicate the profitability of a company's operations. **Purpose of the general ledger and its difference from a subsidiary ledger:**

- The general ledger is the primary accounting record that contains all accounts used by a company, including assets, liabilities, equity, revenue, and expenses.

- It serves as a central repository for recording financial transactions and is organized into individual account balances.
- The general ledger provides a complete and permanent record of all financial activities and is used to prepare financial statements.
- A subsidiary ledger, on the other hand, contains detailed information related to specific accounts in the general ledger.
- Subsidiary ledgers are used to track transactions for individual customers,

suppliers, or specific types of assets or liabilities, providing a more detailed breakdown of account balances.

11. **Explanation of the accounting equation with an example:**

    - The accounting equation, Assets = Liabilities + Equity, represents the fundamental principle of double-entry accounting.
    - Assets are resources owned or controlled by a company, such as cash, inventory, equipment, and property.
    - Liabilities are obligations owed by the company to external parties, such as loans, accounts payable, and accrued expenses.
    - Equity represents the owner's claim on the company's assets after deducting liabilities and reflects the net worth of the business.
    - For example, if a company has assets worth $100,000 and liabilities of $60,000, the equity would be $40,000 ($100,000 - $60,000).

12. **Difference between a balance sheet and an income statement:**

    - A balance sheet provides a snapshot of a company's financial position at a specific point in time, showing its assets, liabilities, and equity.

- It reflects the company's resources (assets) and how those resources are financed (liabilities and equity).

- An income statement, on the other hand, summarizes a company's financial performance over a period of time, typically a month, quarter, or year.
- It shows the company's revenues, expenses, and net income (or net loss) for the period, indicating its profitability.
- While a balance sheet reflects the financial position at a moment, the income statement shows the company's financial performance over a period.

13. **Definition of accounts payable and accounts receivable, and their recording in accounting books:**

    - Accounts payable represent the amounts owed by a company to its suppliers or creditors for goods or services purchased on credit.
    - They are recorded as liabilities on the balance sheet until paid off.
    - Accounts receivable, on the other hand, represent the amounts owed to a company by its customers for goods or services sold on credit.
    - They are recorded as assets on the balance sheet until collected.
    - In accounting books, accounts payable are credited when recorded, while accounts receivable are debited

14. **Significance of the matching principle in accounting:**

- The matching principle requires that expenses be matched with the revenues they help generate in the same accounting period.
- It ensures that the income statement accurately reflects the company's profitability by matching expenses with the revenues they helped generate.
- By matching expenses to the revenues they generate, the matching principle provides a more accurate representation of a company's financial performance.
- It helps avoid distortions in financial reporting and provides stakeholders with reliable information for decision-making.
- The matching principle is fundamental to accrual accounting and is essential for presenting a true and fair view of a company's financial results.

11. **Explanation of inventory valuation methods, such as FIFO and LIFO:**

- FIFO (First-In, First-Out) method assumes that the first items purchased or produced are the first ones sold or used.

- Under FIFO, the cost of goods sold (COGS) is calculated using the cost of the oldest inventory items, while ending inventory is valued using the cost of the most recent purchases.
- LIFO (Last-In, First-Out) method assumes that the most recently purchased or produced items are the first ones sold or used.
- Under LIFO, the cost of goods sold (COGS) is calculated using the cost of the newest inventory items, while ending inventory is valued using the cost of the oldest purchases.
- FIFO results in higher ending inventory values and lower COGS during periods of rising prices, while LIFO has the opposite effect.

12. **Definition of prepaid expenses and their recording in financial statements:**

- Prepaid expenses are costs that have been paid in advance but have not yet been consumed or used up.
- Examples include prepaid rent, prepaid insurance, and prepaid subscriptions.
- Prepaid expenses are recorded as assets on the balance sheet until they are consumed, at which point they are expensed.
- When prepaid expenses are consumed, they are recognized as expenses on the income statement, reducing the company's net income.

13. Calculation of the debt-to-equity ratio and its significance:

- The debt-to-equity ratio is calculated by dividing a company's total debt by its total equity.
- It measures the proportion of a company's financing that comes from debt compared to equity.
- A high debt-to-equity ratio indicates that a company is heavily reliant on debt financing, which may increase financial risk.
- Conversely, a low debt-to-equity ratio suggests that a company relies more on equity financing, which may indicate financial stability.
- The debt-to-equity ratio is used by investors and creditors to assess a company's financial leverage and solvency.

14. Difference between an operating lease and a capital lease:

- An operating lease is a lease agreement in which the lessor retains ownership of the leased asset, and the lessee makes rental payments for the use of the asset.
- Operating leases are typically short-term and do not transfer the risks and rewards of ownership to the lessee.
- A capital lease, also known as a finance lease, transfers substantially all the risks and rewards of ownership to the lessee.

- Capital leases are treated as asset purchases, and the leased asset and corresponding liability are recorded on the lessee's balance sheet.

15. Purpose of the Statement of Cash Flows and its preparation:

- The Statement of Cash Flows provides information about a company's cash inflows and outflows during a specific period.
- It helps investors and creditors assess a company's liquidity, solvency, and ability to generate future cash flows.
- The Statement of Cash Flows is prepared using the indirect method or the direct method.
- The indirect method starts with net income and adjusts for non-cash items and changes in working capital to arrive at the net cash provided by operating activities.
- The direct method directly lists cash receipts and cash payments from operating activities, providing a more detailed breakdown of cash flows.

16. Definition of working capital and its importance in financial management:

- Working capital is the difference between a company's current assets and its current liabilities.
- It represents the funds available for day-to-day operations and indicates a company's short-term liquidity.

- Positive working capital means that a company has more current assets than current liabilities, providing a buffer to meet short-term obligations.
- Negative working capital indicates that a company may struggle to meet its short-term liabilities with its current assets.
- Working capital management is crucial for ensuring smooth operations, managing cash flow, and maintaining financial stability.

17. **Difference between straight-line depreciation and accelerated depreciation methods:**

- Straight-line depreciation allocates an equal amount of depreciation expense to each period of an asset's useful life.
- Accelerated depreciation methods, such as double-declining balance or sum-of-the-years'-digits, allocate more depreciation expense in the early years of an asset's life and less in later years.
- Straight-line depreciation is simpler and results in a consistent expense amount each period.
- Accelerated depreciation methods reflect the assumption that assets lose their value more rapidly in the early years of use.
- Choosing between straight-line and accelerated depreciation depends on factors such as asset usage patterns, tax considerations, and financial reporting requirements.

18. **Calculation of the quick ratio and its interpretation:**
- The quick ratio, also known as the acid-test ratio, is calculated by dividing a company's liquid assets (cash, marketable securities, and accounts receivable) by its current liabilities.
- It measures a company's ability to meet its short-term obligations using its most liquid assets.
- A quick ratio greater than 1 indicates that a company has enough liquid assets to cover its current liabilities.
- A quick ratio less than 1 suggests that a company may struggle to meet its short-term obligations with its liquid assets alone.
- The quick ratio is used by investors, creditors, and analysts to assess a company's short-term liquidity and financial health.

19. **Explanation of financial leverage and its impact on a company's profitability:**
- Financial leverage refers to the use of debt to finance a company's operations and investments.
- It magnifies both profits and losses because interest expense on debt is fixed, while the returns on investments may vary.
- Financial leverage can increase a company's return on equity (ROE) when the return on assets (ROA) exceeds the cost of debt.

- However, excessive financial leverage can also increase financial risk and decrease profitability, especially during economic downturns.
- Finding the right balance of financial leverage is essential for maximizing profitability while managing risk

Definition of amortization and an example of its application:

- Amortization is the process of allocating the cost of intangible assets, such as patents, copyrights, and goodwill, over their useful lives.
- It reflects the gradual consumption or expiration of the asset's economic value over time.
- For example, if a company purchases a patent for $100,000 with a useful life of 10 years, it would amortize $10,000 ($100,000 / 10 years) of the patent's cost each year.
- Amortization expense is recorded on the income statement, reducing the company's net income and taxable income.

21. **Difference between a credit memo and a debit memo:**

- A credit memo is a document issued by a seller to a buyer, indicating that the buyer's account has been credited for a specific amount.
- Credit memos are typically issued for returns, allowances, or discounts granted to customers.
- On the other hand, a debit memo is a document issued by a buyer to a seller, indicating that the buyer's account has been debited for a specific amount.
- Debit memos are often used to request adjustments for overcharges, shortages, or damaged goods.

- While credit memos reduce accounts receivable or revenue for the seller, debit memos increase accounts payable or expenses for the buyer

22. Explanation of revenue recognition and its timing in accounting:

- Revenue recognition is the process of recording revenue in the accounting records when it is earned, regardless of when the cash is received.
- It follows the accrual accounting principle, matching revenues with the expenses they help generate in the same accounting period.
- Revenue is recognized when the following criteria are met: (1) there is persuasive evidence of an arrangement with the customer, (2) delivery has occurred or services have been rendered, (3) the price is fixed or determinable, and (4) collectability is reasonably assured.
- Revenue recognition timing may vary depending on the nature of the transaction, such as sales of goods, rendering of services, or long-term contracts.

23. Calculation of the gross margin ratio and its significance:

- The gross margin ratio, also known as gross profit margin, is calculated by dividing gross profit by total revenue and multiplying by 100 to express it as a percentage.
- Gross profit is the difference between total revenue and the cost of goods sold (COGS).

- The gross margin ratio measures the proportion of each dollar of revenue that represents gross profit, indicating the profitability of a company's core business activities.
- A higher gross margin ratio suggests that a company is more efficient at producing goods or delivering services at a profit.
- The gross margin ratio is used by investors, creditors, and analysts to assess a company's profitability and operating efficiency.

24. **Definition of accrued expenses and accrued revenue:**

- Accrued expenses are expenses that have been incurred but not yet paid or recorded in the accounting records.
- Examples include salaries payable, interest payable, and utilities payable.
- Accrued expenses are recorded as liabilities on the balance sheet and as expenses on the income statement when they are incurred.
- Accrued revenue, on the other hand, represents revenue that has been earned but not yet received or recorded in the accounting records.
- Examples include interest receivable, rent receivable, and services performed but not billed.
- Accrued revenue is recorded as assets on the balance sheet and as revenue on the income statement when it is earned.

25. Description of the process of closing the accounting books at the end of a fiscal period:

- The process of closing the accounting books, also known as the closing process, occurs at the end of the fiscal period to prepare the accounts for the next period.
- It involves transferring the balances of temporary accounts, such as revenue, expenses, and dividends, to the permanent accounts, such as retained earnings.
- The closing process starts by closing revenue accounts to the income summary account and then closing expense accounts to the income summary account.
- Next, the income summary account is closed to retained earnings to update the owner's equity.
- Finally, dividends declared are closed to retained earnings to reflect the distribution of profits to shareholders.
- The closing process ensures that the balances of temporary accounts are zeroed out and ready for the next accounting period, maintaining the accuracy of financial statements.

5. Questions about your strengths, weaknesses, and areas for improvement:

Be prepared to discuss your strengths, weaknesses, and areas for improvement honestly and confidently. Highlight strengths that are relevant to the job and provide examples to support your claims. When discussing weaknesses, focus on how you're actively working to improve or overcome them.

Example: Strength: "One of my strengths is my attention to detail. In my previous role, I was responsible for reconciling accounts, and my meticulous approach helped identify and correct errors before they became significant issues." Weakness: "One area I'm currently working on is public speaking. While I'm comfortable presenting to small groups, I recognize that I could improve my confidence and delivery when speaking in front of larger audiences. To address this weakness, I've been attending public speaking workshops and volunteering for opportunities to practice my presentation skills."

6. Questions about your interest in the company and the role:

Demonstrate your enthusiasm and interest in the company and the role by researching the organization thoroughly before the interview. Tailor your responses to highlight specific aspects of the company's culture, mission, and values that resonate with you. Show how your skills and experiences align with the requirements of the role and how you can contribute to the company's success.

Entry Level Accounting - Interview Guide

Example: Question: "Why are you interested in working for our company?" Answer: "I'm impressed by your company's commitment to innovation and sustainability, as evidenced by your recent initiatives to reduce carbon emissions and invest in renewable energy. I'm particularly excited about the opportunity to contribute to your finance team and support your efforts to drive growth and profitability. I believe my background in financial analysis and reporting aligns well with the requirements of the role, and I'm eager to bring my skills and expertise to your organization."

Conclusion:

Preparing for common interview questions and crafting effective answers can significantly increase your chances of success. Practice answering these questions beforehand and tailor your responses to showcase your skills, experiences, and enthusiasm for the role and the company. With preparation and confidence, you'll be ready to ace your next interview.

Scenario Based Questions

We will cover the most important areas that a interviewer can be interested in assessing your skills

- General accounting
-

Many interviewers prefer to ask scenario- based questions for assessing soft skills. These type of questions effectively help evaluate skills that are not exactly tangible

Scenario based questions - technical knowledge of the accounting profession

1. Title: Recording a Credit Purchase

Scenario: The company receives a large office supply order for $10,000 on credit. How would you record this transaction in the general ledger?

Answer: This transaction would involve two accounts: Office Supplies (an asset account) and Accounts Payable (a liability account). We would debit Office Supplies for $10,000 (to increase the value of office supplies on hand) and credit Accounts Payable for $10,000 (to reflect the company's obligation to pay the supplier).

Entry Level Accounting -Interview Guide

2. Title: Handling a Customer Prepayment

Scenario: A customer pays off a $500 invoice that was previously recorded in accounts receivable. However, they accidentally send a payment of $550. How would you handle the extra $50?

Answer: First, I would credit Accounts Receivable for the original invoice amount of $500. Then, I would record the extra $50 as a customer prepayment. This prepayment can be shown in a separate account within Accounts Receivable or a dedicated customer prepayment account. We would need to contact the customer to clarify their intention for the extra amount and ensure its properly reflected in the accounting records.

3. Title: Accounting for Rent with Landlord Reimbursement

Scenario: The company pays $1,200 for rent each month. This month, an additional $300 was spent on repairs to the office building, which the landlord will reimburse. How would your account for this situation?

Answer: The $1,200 rent payment would be debited to Rent Expense (an expense account) and credited to Cash (an asset account). For the repairs, we would debit Prepaid Rent (an asset account) for $300 because the payment covers future benefits (reimbursement from the landlord). Once the reimbursement is received, we would debit Cash and credit Prepaid Rent for $300

4. Title: Recording Inventory Write-Down

Scenario: Inventory costing $2,000 is accidentally damaged and needs to be written off. Explain the process of recording this in the accounting system.

Answer: We would record this by debiting Inventory Loss (an expense account) for $2,000 and crediting Inventory (an asset account) for $2,000. This reduces the value of inventory on the books to reflect the damaged items. Depending on the company's insurance policy, we might need to follow up with an insurance claim which could involve additional accounting entries.

5. Title: Capitalizing and Depreciating a Delivery Truck

Scenario: The company receives a new delivery truck for $25,000. It will be used for several years. How would you record this on the books?

Answer: The truck is a fixed asset, so we wouldn't record the entire $25,000 as an expense. Instead, we would debit Delivery Truck (an asset account) for $25,000. Over the useful life of the truck, we would record depreciation expense by debiting Depreciation Expense (an expense account) and crediting Accumulated Depreciation-Delivery Truck (a contra asset account). This process spreads the cost of the truck over its useful life.

Entry Level Accounting -Interview Guide

6. Title: Explaining Cash Flow vs. Net Income to a Client

Scenario: A client inquiry about the difference between cash flow and net income. How would you explain it in a clear and concise way?

Answer: I would explain that net income reflects the company's profitability over a period by considering all revenues and expenses, regardless of whether cash is received or paid. Cash flow, on the other hand, focuses on the actual movement of cash in and out of the business. Net income might include transactions where cash hasn't been exchanged yet (e.g., accounts receivable and payable), while cash flow only considers actual cash receipts and disbursements.

7. Title: Accounting for Stock Issuance

Scenario: The company issues 1,000 shares of common stock for $10 per share. How would you record this transaction?

Answer: This transaction increases the company's equity. We would debit Cash (an asset account) for $10,000 (1,000 shares x $10 per share) and credit Common Stock (a stockholders' equity account) for $10,000.

8. Title: Reconciling a Petty Cash Discrepancy

Scenario: You notice a discrepancy between the bank statement and the company's accounting records for petty cash. How would you approach resolving this issue?

Answer: I would perform a bank reconciliation. This process involves comparing the company's petty cash ledger with the

9. Title: Understanding Accruals vs. Prepayments

Scenario: Explain the difference between accruals and prepayments in accounting.

Answer: Accruals and prepayments are both temporary accounts used to recognize expenses or revenue before the cash is paid or received. However, they differ in timing:

- **Accruals:** These represent expenses incurred but not yet paid or revenue earned but not yet collected. For example, if you receive services in December but the invoice isn't received until January, you would accrue an expense in December.
- **Prepayments:** These represent expenses paid for in advance or revenue collected before it's earned. For instance, if you pay rent for the entire year in January, you would record a prepaid rent asset in January and gradually expense it throughout the year.

10. Title: Journalizing Bank Account Activity

Scenario: The company's bank statement shows a deposit of $1,500, a service charge of $10, and an outstanding check of $700. What journal entries would you make to record this information?

Entry Level Accounting - Interview Guide

Answer: We would make three separate journal entries:

1. **Deposit:** Debit Cash (for $1,500) and Credit Sales Revenue (or another appropriate revenue account) for $1,500 (assuming the deposit represents a customer payment).
2. **Service Charge:** Debit Bank Service Charge (an expense account) for $10 and Credit Cash for $10 (to reflect the fee deducted by the bank).
3. **Outstanding Check:** Debit Accounts Payable (or another appropriate liability account) for $700 and Credit Cash for $700 (to recognize the liability for the check that hasn't cleared yet).

These entries ensure the company's accounting records accurately reflect the bank account activity.

10 Scenario Based Questions -Attention to Details

These questions are designed to assess the candidate's ability to identify and process specific details within an accounting scenario.

1. Title: Missing Information in an Invoice

Scenario: You receive an invoice for office supplies for $500. However, the due date is missing. What steps would you take to ensure proper processing?

Answer: I would first contact the supplier to clarify the missing due date. This information is crucial for accurate recordkeeping and timely payments. I would document the date and details of the communication for future reference.

2. Title: Discrepancy in Inventory Count

Scenario: During a physical inventory count, you discover that there are 10 more boxes of printer paper than what's recorded in the system. How would you handle this situation?

Answer: I would first double-check my count to ensure accuracy. Then, I would investigate the discrepancy by reviewing recent purchase orders and receiving reports. I would document the investigation process and adjust the inventory records accordingly. If the cause remains unclear, I might need to consult with a supervisor for further guidance.

3. Title: Incorrect Account Number on a Check

Scenario: You are preparing a check for a vendor payment but notice a typo in their account number. How would you proceed?

Answer: I would stop processing the check immediately. I would then contact the vendor to verify the correct account number. It's crucial to ensure the funds reach the intended recipient to avoid delays and potential penalties.

4. Title: Customer Payment Exceeds Invoice Amount

Scenario: A customer sends a payment of $220 for an invoice that is only $200. What would you do?

Entry Level Accounting -Interview Guide

Answer: I would first research the customer's account to see if they have any outstanding invoices. If no outstanding balance exists, I would contact the customer to confirm their intention for the extra $20. It could be an overpayment or a prepayment for a future purchase. I would document the communication and ensure the customer's records are updated accordingly.

5. Title: Missing Receipt for Petty Cash Reimbursement

Scenario: An employee submits a petty cash reimbursement request with all receipts except for a $10 office supply purchase. What would you do?

Answer: I would request the missing receipt from the employee. Petty cash reimbursements require proper documentation for all expenses. Without the receipt, I would need to hold off on processing the full reimbursement until the documentation is provided.

6. Title: Encoding Error in a Journal Entry

Scenario: You review a journal entry for a purchase and notice the amount is accidentally entered as $1,570 instead of $1,750. How would you correct this error?

Answer: I would identify the specific error (incorrect amount) and document the mistake. Depending on the accounting software used, there might be a correction function or I would need to prepare a reversing entry to negate the original incorrect entry, followed by a new entry with the accurate amount.

7. Title: Unfamiliar Transaction Code on a Bank Statement

Scenario: You are reconciling the bank statement and encounter a transaction code you don't recognize. How would you research this unfamiliar code?

Answer: I would consult the bank statement legend or contact the bank directly to inquire about the meaning of the unfamiliar code. Understanding the transaction nature is crucial for accurate bank reconciliation.

8. Title: Duplicate Invoice Processing

Scenario: A vendor accidentally sends you the same invoice twice. How would you identify and prevent duplicate payment?

Answer: I would carefully examine the invoice details, including the invoice number and date. Accounting software often has features to flag duplicate invoices. I would then contact the vendor to confirm the situation and ensure only one payment is processed.

9. Title: Canceled Check Not Reflected in Bank Statement

Scenario: You know a check was voided and reissued, but the bank statement still shows the original canceled check. How would you handle this discrepancy?

Entry Level Accounting -Interview Guide

Answer: This might be a timing issue where the bank hasn't yet processed the cancellation. I would reconcile the bank statement based on the actual outstanding checks and document the situation for future reference. It might be necessary to follow up with the bank if the discrepancy persists.

10. Title: Missing Decimal Point in a General Ledger Account

Scenario: You suspect an error in a general ledger account because the balance seems unusually high. Upon closer inspection, you discover a missing decimal point. How would you correct this error?

Answer: I would identify the specific error (missing decimal) and document the mistake. Depending on the accounting software, there might be a correction function, or I would need to adjust the

10 Scenario Based Questions - Potential for Leadership

These questions aim to assess the candidate's ability to think strategically, influence others, and potentially lead within the accounting team.

1. Title: Standardizing Processes for Efficiency

Shahida J.

Scenario: You notice inconsistencies in how team members handle petty cash reimbursements. How would you approach standardizing the process to improve efficiency?

Answer: I would first observe the different approaches and identify areas for improvement. Then, I would research best practices for petty cash management. Next, I would collaborate with colleagues to develop a clear and consistent procedure for reimbursement requests and documentation. I would present the proposed process to the team, highlighting the benefits of standardization (e.g., time savings, reduced errors).

2. Title: Identifying and Mentoring a Junior Team Member

Scenario: You observe a new team member struggling with a specific accounting task. How would you offer support and guidance?

Answer: I would first approach the team member in a friendly and helpful manner. I would offer to explain the task again, breaking it down into smaller steps. I would encourage them to ask questions and be open to feedback. Depending on the complexity, I might suggest creating a training document or resource sheet for future reference.

Entry Level Accounting - Interview Guide

3. Title: Leading a Team Brainstorming Session

Scenario: Your team is tasked with identifying ways to reduce accounting software errors. How would you lead a brainstorming session to generate ideas?

Answer: I would start by clearly defining the problem and desired outcome. To encourage participation, I would create a welcoming and inclusive atmosphere. I would use brainstorming techniques like mind-mapping or round-robin discussions to capture a variety of ideas. I would actively listen to suggestions and acknowledge everyone's contribution.

4. Title: Delegating Tasks Effectively

Scenario: You are assigned a large project with a tight deadline. How would you delegate tasks effectively to your team members?

Answer: I would first evaluate the project scope and identify specific tasks that can be delegated. I would then consider each team member's strengths and weaknesses when assigning tasks. I would provide clear instructions, deadlines, and resources needed to complete the assigned tasks. I would also schedule regular check-in meetings to answer questions and monitor progress.

5. Title: Resolving Conflict Between Team Members

Scenario: You observe two team members disagreeing on the proper accounting treatment for a specific transaction. How would you intervene and facilitate a resolution?

Answer: I would first separate the team members to de-escalate any tension. Then, I would encourage them to calmly explain their perspectives on the issue. I would ask clarifying questions to fully understand their reasoning. By referring to accounting standards or consulting with a supervisor, I would help them find a solution that adheres to proper accounting principles.

6. Title: Identifying Training Needs and Solutions

Scenario: You recognize that a team member could benefit from training in a specific accounting software program. How would you approach this situation?

Answer: I would first discuss the training need with the team member and assess their current skill level. I would then research available training options, considering online courses, in-person workshops, or self-study materials. I would present the different options to the team member and work collaboratively to choose the most suitable training method.

7. Title: Presenting Complex Accounting Information to Non-Financial Professionals

Scenario: You are tasked with explaining a new accounting policy change to a group of managers who lack a financial background. How would you prepare and deliver the presentation?

Answer: I would anticipate the audience's level of understanding and avoid using overly technical jargon. I would focus on the key points and how the new policy affects their work. I would prepare visual aids such as charts and graphs to enhance clarity. I would encourage questions throughout the presentation and be prepared to explain concepts in a simple and concise manner.

8. Title: Motivating a Team During Difficult Periods

Scenario: The team is facing a heavy workload and morale seems low. How would you motivate and encourage your colleagues?

Answer: I would acknowledge the pressure and workload the team is facing. I would express appreciation for their hard work and dedication. I would work with the team to identify areas where tasks can be redistributed or deadlines adjusted. I might suggest small team-building exercises or breaks to boost morale and maintain focus.

9. Title: Identifying Opportunities for Process Improvement

Scenario: You believe there is a more efficient way to handle a specific accounting task. How would you propose the change to your supervisor?

Answer: I would gather data and evidence to support your claim about the current process's inefficiencies. You could research best practices or benchmark against other companies. Prepare a clear and concise proposal outlining the proposed change, the associated

Shahida J.

10. Title: Promoting Collaboration Across Departments

Scenario: You suspect that there might be a communication gap between the accounting department and another department (e.g., sales or marketing). How would you initiate collaboration to improve communication and overall efficiency?

Answer: I would first identify the specific department where communication seems lacking. Then, I would research common communication gaps between accounting and other departments. I would reach out to a colleague in the other department and initiate a conversation to understand their perspective and challenges. I would propose solutions like setting up regular inter-departmental meetings, creating shared documents or dashboards, or developing a communication protocol for specific tasks. By fostering collaboration, you can streamline processes and improve overall organizational efficiency.

Entry Level Accounting -Interview Guide

10 Scenario Based Questions - Working in Pressure Situations

1. Title: Meeting a Tight Deadline with Limited Resources

Scenario: You are assigned a critical report with a very tight deadline. You are also facing a high workload with other tasks. How would you manage your time and resources to ensure the report is completed on time and to a high standard?

Answer: I would first prioritize the tasks and clearly identify the most critical elements of the report. I would then create a detailed schedule, allocating time for research, data analysis, writing, and proofreading. I would communicate the deadline and potential resource limitations to my supervisor and seek any possible support or delegation opportunities. Effectively managing my time, prioritizing tasks, and communicating proactively would help me deliver the report efficiently.

2. Title: Handling Unexpected Errors During Data Entry

Scenario: You are entering a large amount of data into the accounting system and discover several errors halfway through. How would you approach correcting the errors while minimizing disruption to the workflow?

Answer: First, I would document the identified errors, including the specific data points and their discrepancies. Then, I would back up the data entry so far to ensure a safe retrieval point in case of further complications. I would consult with a supervisor or a more experienced team member to determine the best course of action for correcting the errors. This might involve re-entering specific entries or utilizing data correction tools within the accounting software. Finally, I would implement additional verification steps to minimize the risk of similar errors in the future.

3. Title: Responding to Client Inquiries During Tax Season

Scenario: You are working in a busy tax season and receive a call from a client with an urgent question about their tax return. How would you manage the inquiry while ensuring other client deadlines are met?

Answer: I would prioritize the client's call and address their question efficiently. I would actively listen to their concern and ask clarifying questions to fully understand the issue. Based on the urgency of the question, I might offer immediate guidance or schedule a follow-up call for a more detailed explanation. I would also communicate clearly with the client about any potential delays and manage their expectations. Maintaining clear communication and prioritizing tasks would be essential under pressure

4. Title: Dealing with System Outages or Software Issues

Scenario: You are working on a critical task when the accounting software experiences a technical issue. How would you react and proceed?

Answer: I would first remain calm and assess the situation. If the issue is minor, I might try restarting the software or clearing the cache to see if it resolves itself. If the software remains unavailable, I would document the issue and attempt to recreate it for future troubleshooting purposes. I would then focus on completing tasks that don't require the software or utilize alternative methods for data capture. Additionally, I would report the outage to the IT department or a designated support team to expedite a resolution.

5. Title: Working Effectively Under Pressure from Management

Scenario: You are nearing a deadline for a complex accounting project and your supervisor is putting pressure on you to complete it quickly. How would you handle this situation?

Answer: I would acknowledge your supervisor's concern and explain the progress made on the project so far. If there are any roadblocks or potential delays, I would communicate them clearly and proactively seek guidance or resources that might be needed. I might suggest breaking down the remaining tasks into smaller, more manageable steps to demonstrate your commitment to meeting the deadline. Maintaining open communication and focusing on solutions would help manage the pressure effectively.

6. Title: Managing Multiple Deadlines and Projects Simultaneously

Scenario: You are juggling multiple projects with conflicting deadlines. How would you prioritize your workload and ensure high-quality work on all tasks?

Answer: I would create a comprehensive list of all deadlines and tasks. I would then prioritize them based on urgency and importance. I would estimate the time needed for each task and create a realistic schedule. Utilizing project management tools or a calendar system with reminders would help maintain organization. Furthermore, I would leverage time management techniques like focusing on one task at a time while taking short breaks to avoid burnout.

7. Title: Resolving a Disagreement with a Client Over Billing

Scenario: A client disputes the accuracy of an invoice you sent them. How would you approach this situation and resolve the discrepancy?

Answer: I would first maintain a professional demeanor and acknowledge the client's concern. I would then review the invoice details and the underlying accounting records. I would be prepared to explain the charges and provide supporting documentation. If a mistake is identified, I would apologize for the error and promptly issue a corrected invoice

Entry Level Accounting -Interview Guide

8. Title: Handling Unexpected Questions During a Presentation

Scenario: You are delivering a presentation on a new accounting policy to a group of colleagues. They interrupt you with several unexpected questions. How would you manage the situation and ensure the presentation stays on track?

Answer: I would acknowledge the questions and politely ask if they can wait until the end of the presentation for a more detailed response. This allows me to maintain the flow of the presentation and ensures everyone gets the key points first. I would also take notes on the questions to ensure they are addressed later. If a question is particularly relevant to the current topic, I might briefly address it without derailing the overall presentation structure. Finally, at the designated time, I would revisit the questions and provide clear and concise answers.

9. Title: Maintaining Composure When Dealing with an Angry Customer

Scenario: You receive a call from an upset customer who is frustrated about a late payment. How would you de-escalate the situation and address their concerns?

Answer: I would first remain calm and listen attentively to the customer's complaint. Acknowledge their frustration and apologize for any inconvenience caused. I would then ask clarifying questions to understand the specific issue. Once I have a better understanding, I would explain the situation clearly and professionally.

If possible, I would offer solutions or next steps to resolve the problem. Throughout the interaction, I would maintain a respectful and empathetic tone to de-escalate the situation and ensure a positive outcome.

10. Title: Adapting to Sudden Changes in Work Priorities

Scenario: You are working on a specific task when your supervisor assigns you a new, urgent priority. How would you manage this change and ensure both tasks are completed effectively?

Answer: I would first acknowledge the new priority and ask for clarification on the urgency and deadline. I would then assess my current workload and communicate potential delays with the original task if necessary. Depending on the complexity of both tasks, I might delegate some aspects of the original task or negotiate a revised deadline. Demonstrating flexibility and adaptability while effectively communicating with your supervisor would be crucial in smoothly handling this situation.

10 Scenario Based Questions - Ability to think 5-years Ahead

These questions assess the candidate's ability to think strategically and consider long-term implications of accounting decisions.

1. Title: Potential Impact of Technological Advancements

Entry Level Accounting -Interview Guide

Scenario: How do you see technological advancements impacting the accounting field in the next five years? How might this change your approach to your work?

Answer: I foresee advancements like artificial intelligence (AI) and machine learning automating repetitive tasks like data entry and reconciliation. This would free up accountants to focus on more analytical and strategic tasks, such as financial modeling and risk assessment. I would need to stay updated on these technologies and be prepared to adapt my skillset to leverage them effectively.

2. Title: Considering Future Business Growth

Scenario: The company is experiencing rapid growth. How would you ensure the accounting department's practices and systems can accommodate this expansion in the next few years?

Answer: I would recommend conducting a scalability assessment of the current accounting software and processes. If necessary, I would explore options for upgrading the software to handle increased transaction volume. Additionally, I would suggest developing a system for documenting and standardizing accounting procedures to ensure consistency as the team grows.

3. Title: Anticipating Changes in Accounting Standards

Answer: I would stay informed about upcoming changes in accounting standards (e.g., new International Financial Reporting Standards - IFRS) and their potential impact on the company's financial reporting. I would proactively research and understand these changes to ensure the accounting department is prepared to implement them smoothly.

Scenario: Regulatory bodies might introduce new accounting standards in the future. How would you stay prepared and ensure the company's compliance?

4. Title: Assessing Long-Term Implications of Business Decisions

Scenario: The company is considering a major investment in a new product line. How would you analyze the financial feasibility of this project from a long-term perspective?

Answer: I would go beyond the initial investment cost and consider factors like projected revenue growth, operational expenses, return on investment (ROI), and potential risks associated with the new product line. By analyzing long-term financial data and trends, I could provide insights to support informed decision-making.

5. Title: Envisioning Future Career Development

Scenario: Where do you see yourself within the accounting field in the next five years? How can this company support your career aspirations?

Answer: I am interested in specializing in [mention a specific area of accounting, e.g., forensic accounting or tax accounting]. I would seek opportunities within the company to gain experience in that area, such as shadowing senior accountants or participating in relevant training programs.

This company's commitment to employee development would be a major factor in my decision to stay and grow my career here.

6. Title: Considering Automation's Impact on Job Roles

Scenario: As accounting tasks become automated, how do you see the role of accountants evolving? What skills would become crucial for success?

Answer: While automation might handle routine tasks, accountants will still be needed for their analytical and problem-solving skills. In the future, strong communication, critical thinking, and the ability to interpret complex financial data will be even more important for success.

7. Title: Identifying Opportunities for Cost Reduction

Scenario: If tasked with reducing accounting department expenses in the next five years, what strategies would you consider?

Answer: I would explore ways to improve efficiency by automating repetitive tasks or streamlining existing processes. I would also research potential cost savings in areas like software subscriptions or outsourcing non-core accounting functions. However, cost reduction shouldn't compromise accuracy or data security.

8. Title: Forecasting Future Financial Trends

Scenario: How can an understanding of historical financial data help predict future trends for the company?

Answer: By analyzing trends in revenue, expenses, and profitability over time, we can identify patterns and forecast future financial performance. This information is crucial for budgeting, resource allocation, and making strategic business decisions.

9. Title: Assessing Potential Risks and Opportunities in New Markets

Scenario: The company is considering expanding into a new market. What financial risks and opportunities would you consider when analyzing this decision?

Answer: I would research the new market's economic climate, tax regulations, and potential currency fluctuations. Understanding these factors would help identify potential risks like currency exchange losses or economic instability. Additionally, I would assess the projected profitability and growth potential in the new market.

10. Title: Adapting Accounting Practices to Changing Economic Conditions

Scenario: Economic conditions can fluctuate significantly over time. How can the accounting department adapt its practices to ensure continued accuracy and relevance during periods of economic change (e.g., recession or inflation)?

Answer: Here are some ways the accounting department can adapt its practices to changing economic conditions:

- **Inventory Valuation Methods:** During periods of inflation, it might be necessary to re-evaluate inventory valuation methods to reflect the increased cost of replacing goods. Considering methods like LIFO (Last-In, First-Out) could provide a more accurate representation of current inventory value.

- **Bad Debt Allowance Adjustments:** In an economic downturn, the risk of bad debt (uncollectable accounts receivable) increases. The accounting department should reassess and potentially adjust the bad debt allowance to account for the higher risk of defaults.

- **Forecasting and Scenario Planning:** Developing financial forecasts under different economic scenarios (optimistic, pessimistic) allows for better planning and resource allocation. This proactive approach helps the company adapt to changing economic conditions while minimizing financial risks.

- **Communication and Transparency:** Maintaining clear communication with management regarding the potential impact of economic changes on the company's finances is crucial. Transparency allows for informed decision-making and helps mitigate potential risks.

- **Focus on Long-Term Sustainability:** The accounting department can play a vital role in driving long-term financial sustainability by emphasizing cost control measures and identifying areas for operational efficiency gains. This strengthens the company's resilience during economic downturns.

By adapting practices and focusing on long-term sustainability, the accounting department can ensure its work remains accurate and relevant even in a changing economic landscape.

10 Scenario Based Questions – Working in Teams

1. **Handling Conflicting Opinions Scenario:** During a team meeting, two of your colleagues had a disagreement over the best approach to reconcile a complex set of financial records. How would you handle this situation? Answer: I would first listen to both perspectives and try to understand the reasoning behind their differing opinions. Then, I would suggest taking a step back and reviewing the relevant data and accounting principles objectively. If needed, I would propose involving a senior team member or manager to provide guidance and help reach a resolution that aligns with best practices and the organization's policies.

2. **Collaborating with Cross-Functional Teams Scenario:** As an accountant, you may need to work closely with teams from other departments, such as IT or marketing. How would you approach collaborating with cross-functional teams to ensure effective communication and alignment? Answer: I understand the importance of effective collaboration across different departments. I would first take the time to understand the goals and priorities of the cross-functional team, as well as any specific terminology or processes they follow. I would then clearly communicate the accounting perspective and requirements, ensuring that everyone is on the same page. Throughout the collaboration, I would maintain open lines of communication, actively listen to their inputs, and

work together to find solutions that meet the needs of all parties involved.

3. **Managing Deadlines and Priorities Scenario:** You and your team are working on a tight deadline for a financial reporting project, but one team member is falling behind due to personal reasons. How would you handle this situation while ensuring the team meets the deadline? Answer: I would approach the situation with empathy and understanding, as personal circumstances can sometimes affect work performance. First, I would have a one-on-one conversation with the team member to understand their situation better and offer any support or resources they may need. Then, I would work closely with the team to redistribute tasks and prioritize the most critical deliverables to meet the deadline. If necessary, I would suggest seeking an extension or interim deadline from the stakeholders, ensuring transparency and open communication throughout the process.

4. **Providing Constructive Feedback Scenario:** During a team project, you notice that one of your team members is consistently making errors in their work, which could potentially impact the accuracy of the financial reports. How would you approach providing constructive feedback to help them improve? Answer: I would schedule a private meeting with the team member to discuss my

observations and concerns. I would approach the situation with empathy and a focus on improvement, avoiding personal criticism or accusatory language. I would provide specific examples of the errors and explain how they could impact the team's work and the organization. Together, we would identify potential root causes and develop an action plan to address any knowledge gaps or process improvements needed. Throughout this process, I would offer my support

5. encourage an open dialogue to ensure the feedback is received positively and leads to tangible improvements

6. **Embracing Diverse Perspectives Scenario:** Your team consists of individuals from diverse cultural and educational backgrounds. How would you ensure that everyone's perspectives and contributions are valued and incorporated into the team's work? Answer: I believe that diversity in perspectives can greatly enrich the team's work and lead to more well-rounded solutions. I would actively encourage an environment of inclusivity and respect, where everyone feels comfortable sharing their ideas and opinions without fear of judgment or discrimination. During team meetings or discussions, I would make a conscious effort to

solicit input from all team members, ensuring that no one's voice is overlooked. I would also be mindful of potential cultural differences or communication styles and strive to create a safe space for open and respectful dialogue.

7. **Resolving Conflicts and Disagreements Scenario:** During a team project, two of your colleagues have a heated disagreement over the appropriate accounting treatment for a complex transaction. How would you approach resolving this conflict and maintaining a positive team dynamic? Answer: In situations of conflict, I would first aim to defuse any tensions by encouraging both parties to take a step back and approach the discussion with a calm and professional demeanor.

8. I would then facilitate an open and respectful dialogue, ensuring that each person has the opportunity to voice their perspective

9. and reasoning without interruption. If needed, I would suggest consulting relevant accounting standards, guidelines, or subject matter experts to gain a deeper understanding of the issue at hand. Throughout the process, I would remain impartial and focus on finding a resolution that aligns with

best practices and the organization's policies, while also considering the team's collective input and expertise.

10. Delegating Tasks and Responsibilities Scenario:

As part of a team project, you need to delegate specific tasks and responsibilities to your team members. How would you approach this process to ensure fair distribution of work and effective collaboration? Answer: When delegating tasks and responsibilities, I would first assess the strengths, experiences, and workloads of each team member. I would then clearly outline the project goals, deadlines, and expectations to ensure everyone is on the same page. Based on this information, I would assign tasks and responsibilities in a fair and balanced manner, considering each individual's skills and capacity. Throughout the process, I would maintain open communication and provide opportunities for team members to provide input or express any concerns. I would also establish regular check-ins and progress updates to ensure tasks are being completed on time and to address any challenges or roadblocks that may arise.

11. Encouraging Continuous Learning Scenario:
During a team meeting, one of your colleagues expresses interest in learning a new accounting software or technique that could benefit the team's

productivity. How would you support and encourage continuous learning within the team?
Answer: I strongly believe in the importance of continuous learning and professional development, as it not only benefits the individual but also the entire team and organization.

In this scenario, I would first commend my colleague for their initiative and eagerness to learn. I would then explore opportunities for formal training or workshops related to the desired software or technique, and advocate for the team to attend or allocate time for self-study.

12. Additionally, I would encourage knowledge sharing within the team, where those who have expertise in certain areas could provide informal training or mentorship to others. By fostering a culture of continuous learning, we can collectively improve our skills, stay up-to-date with industry trends, and enhance our overall effectiveness as a team.

13. **Celebrating Team Successes Scenario:** Your team has successfully completed a major financial reporting project ahead of schedule and with excellent quality. How would you celebrate this achievement and recognize the team's efforts?

Answer: Celebrating team successes is essential for boosting morale, fostering a positive team dynamic, and acknowledging the hard work and dedication of each individual. In this scenario, I would first express my sincere appreciation and gratitude to the entire team, highlighting the collective effort and commitment that led to the successful outcome. I would then propose a team celebration, such as a group lunch or team-building activity, to provide an opportunity for everyone to unwind and enjoy each other's company outside of the work setting.

During this celebration, I would make a point to recognize and commend specific contributions or exceptional efforts from individual team members. By celebrating team successes, we not only build camaraderie but also reinforce a culture of recognition and appreciation.

14. **Embracing Change and Adaptability Scenario:** Your organization is implementing a new accounting software system, which will require your team to adapt to new processes and workflows. How would you approach this change and ensure your team remains productive and efficient during the transition? Answer: Change can be challenging, but it also presents an opportunity for growth and improvement. In this scenario, I would first acknowledge the potential disruption and concerns that may arise from the

team regarding the new software implementation. I would then work closely with the team to clearly understand the new system's features, capabilities, and expected benefits. Together, we would develop a comprehensive training plan and establish dedicated time for everyone to familiarize themselves with the new software and processes. During the transition, I would encourage open communication and regularly check in with team members to address any issues or challenges they may be facing.

Additionally, I would foster a mindset of adaptability and continuous improvement, emphasizing the long-term benefits and efficiencies the new system will bring to our workflows. By embracing change with a positive and proactive approach, we can navigate the transition smoothly and ensure our team remains productive and effective throughout the process

Chapter 4: Asking Insightful Questions

Interviews are a two-way street, and while the interviewer's primary goal is to assess your suitability for the role, it's equally important for you to gather information and gain insights into the company, team, and position. Asking meaningful questions not only demonstrates your genuine interest and engagement but also helps you determine whether the opportunity aligns with your career goals and aspirations.

Examples of Good Questions that would be asked about the company, team, and role:

1. Company Culture and Values:
    - "Can you describe the company's culture and core values?"
    - "How does the organization promote work-life balance and employee well-being?"
    - "What initiatives or programs does the company have in place to support diversity, equity, and inclusion?"
2. Team Dynamics and Collaboration:
    - "Can you provide insight into the team structure and how different roles collaborate?"
    - "What are the team's biggest strengths, and what areas are you currently focused on improving?"
    - "How does the team foster open communication and knowledge sharing?"

Entry Level Accounting -Interview Guide

3. Growth and Development Opportunities:
   - "What professional development opportunities are available for entry-level accountants?"
   - "Can you describe the potential career paths within the accounting department or organization?"
   - "How does the company support continuous learning and upskilling of its employees?"
4. Challenges and Priorities:
   - "What are the main challenges or priorities the accounting team is currently facing?"
   - "How does the team approach problem-solving and continuous improvement initiatives?"
   - "Can you provide an example of a recent successful project or initiative the accounting team has undertaken?"
5. Day-to-Day Responsibilities:
   - "Can you walk me through a typical day or week in this role?"
   - "What would be my primary responsibilities and key areas of focus in the first few months?"
   - "How is performance measured and evaluated for this position?"

Questions to Avoid Asking During an Interview:

1. Salary and Benefits (initially):

- It's generally advisable to avoid discussing compensation and benefits too early in the interview process unless the interviewer brings it up first.
2. Overly Specific or Hypothetical Questions:
    - Avoid asking questions that are too specific or based on hypothetical situations, as the interviewer may not have enough context to provide a meaningful answer.
3. Personal or Inappropriate Questions:
    - Refrain from asking personal questions about the interviewer or inquiring about topics that could be considered inappropriate or sensitive.
4. Questions That Could Be Easily Answered Through Research:
    - Avoid asking basic questions about the company or role that could have been answered through research on the company's website or job description.

By asking thoughtful and relevant questions, you demonstrate your preparedness, intellectual curiosity, and genuine interest in the opportunity.

Chapter 5: Following Up After the Interview

Following Up After the Interview

The interview process doesn't end when you leave the room or hang up the call. The actions you take after the interview can significantly impact your chances of securing the position or leaving a lasting positive impression, even if you don't get the job this time around.

Writing a Thank-You Note and Its Significance

A well-crafted thank-you note is a courteous and professional gesture that can set you apart from other candidates. It serves several important purposes:

1. Expressing Gratitude: A thank-you note allows you to express your appreciation for the interviewer's time and consideration, reinforcing your interest in the role.
2. Reiterating Your Qualifications: While keeping it concise, you can reiterate key points that highlight your suitability for the position, or address any additional strengths or experiences you may have forgotten to mention during the interview.
3. Demonstrating Professionalism: A thoughtful thank-you note reflects your attention to detail, communication skills, and commitment to following through, which are qualities valued in the accounting profession.

When writing a thank-you note, aim for a tone that is sincere, respectful, and professional. If you interviewed with multiple people, consider sending individual notes to each interviewer, personalizing each one with specific details from your conversation. While email is generally acceptable, a handwritten note can add a touch of thoughtfulness and make a lasting impression.

Evaluating Your Performance and Identifying Areas for Improvement

After the interview, take some time to reflect on your performance and identify areas where you excelled and areas where you could improve. This self-evaluation process can help you refine your interviewing skills and better prepare for future opportunities.

Consider the following questions:

- How well did you articulate your qualifications and experiences?
- Were you able to effectively communicate your interest and enthusiasm for the role?
- Did you ask insightful questions that demonstrated your understanding of the company and position?
- How was your body language and overall presence during the interview?
- Were there any questions or scenarios that caught you off guard, and how could you better prepare for those in the future?

Entry Level Accounting -Interview Guide

Seek feedback from trusted friends, family members, or career advisors who may have helped you practice or conduct mock interviews. Their outside perspectives can provide valuable insights into areas where you shone and areas that could use improvement.

Handling Job Offers and Negotiations (if applicable)

If you receive a job offer, congratulations! This is an exciting milestone, but it's important to approach the next steps thoughtfully and professionally.

1. Expressing Gratitude and Enthusiasm: When receiving the offer, express your sincere gratitude and enthusiasm for the opportunity. Even if you need time to consider the offer, convey your appreciation and interest in a positive manner.
2. Reviewing the Offer Details: Carefully review the written offer, including the compensation package, benefits, and any other terms or conditions. If anything is unclear or requires clarification, don't hesitate to ask questions.
3. Negotiating (if desired): If you wish to negotiate any aspects of the offer, such as salary or benefits, do so respectfully and with a collaborative mindset. Present your case objectively, citing relevant market data or your specific qualifications and experiences that support your request.
4. Providing a Timely Response: Whether you choose to accept or decline the offer, provide a timely response within the agreed-upon timeframe. If you need additional time to consider the offer, communicate this professionally and provide a reasonable timeline for your decision.

5. Graciously Declining (if applicable): If you decide to decline the offer, express your gratitude for the opportunity and consideration. You may choose to provide a brief and professional explanation for your decision, but avoid burning bridges or speaking negatively about the company or role.

Remember, the way you handle job offers and negotiations can significantly impact your professional reputation and future opportunities within the industry.

By following up professionally after the interview, you not only increase your chances of securing the desired position but also demonstrate the qualities and professionalism that are highly valued in the accounting field.

Chapter 6: Additional Tips and Resources

While the previous chapters have focused on preparing for and excelling in the interview process, your journey as an aspiring accountant doesn't end there. Continuous learning, professional development, and networking are essential for long-term success and growth in the accounting field. This chapter provides additional tips and resources to help you build a solid foundation and stay ahead in your career.

Networking and Building Professional Relationships

Networking is a crucial aspect of career development, and it's never too early to start building meaningful professional relationships. Here are some tips for effective networking:

1. Attend industry events and conferences: Participate in local or national accounting events, conferences, and seminars. These gatherings provide opportunities to meet professionals in your field, learn about industry trends, and potentially find job or internship opportunities.
2. Join professional associations: Consider joining organizations like the American Institute of CPAs (AICPA), your state CPA society, or other relevant accounting associations. These groups often host networking events, workshops, and offer valuable resources for members.

3. Leverage your university's resources: Connect with your university's career center, alumni network, and professors. They can provide guidance, introductions, and insights into the accounting profession.

4. Utilize social media: Platforms like LinkedIn can be powerful networking tools. Build a professional online presence, connect with colleagues and industry leaders, and engage in relevant discussions.
5. Informational interviews: Reach out to professionals in your desired field and request informational interviews. These conversations can provide valuable insights into different career paths and help you build relationships within the industry.

Remember, networking is about building genuine connections and adding value to others. Approach it with a mindset of learning, sharing knowledge, and mutual growth.

Continuing Education and Professional Development Opportunities

The accounting profession is constantly evolving, and it's essential to stay up-to-date with industry changes, regulations, and best practices. Here are some opportunities for continuing education and professional development:

Entry Level Accounting - Interview Guide

1. Certifications and credentials: Pursue certifications like the Certified Public Accountant (CPA), Certified Management Accountant (CMA), or Certified Internal Auditor (CIA) to enhance your knowledge and credibility in the field.
2. Graduate studies: Consider pursuing a master's degree in accounting, taxation, or a related field to deepen your expertise and potentially specialize in a specific area.
3. Professional development courses: Enroll in courses, seminars, or workshops offered by professional organizations, universities, or online platforms to expand your skillset and stay current with industry trends.
4. On-the-job training: Seek out opportunities for mentorship, job shadowing, or rotational programs within your organization to learn from experienced professionals and gain practical experience.
5. Self-study and research: Stay informed by reading industry publications, journals, and keeping up with regulatory changes and best practices in the accounting field.

Recommended Books, Websites, and Other Resources

To further support your professional growth and development, here are some recommended books, websites, and other resources for aspiring accountants:

Books:

1. "Financial Intelligence" by Karen Berman and Joe Knight
2. "The Accounting Game" by Darrell Mullis and Judith Orloff
3. "The Lean Accounting Guidebook" by Steven M. Bragg
4. "The Accounting Career Launch" by Hugh Cram and Abdul Khan

Websites and Online Resources:

1. Journal of Accountancy (www.journalofaccountancy.com)
2. Accounting Today (www.accountingtoday.com)
3. AccountingCoach (www.accountingcoach.com)
4. Accounting.com (www.accounting.com)
5. Coursera and edX (for online accounting courses and certifications)

Entry Level Accounting -Interview Guide

Professional Organizations:

1. American Institute of CPAs (AICPA) (www.aicpa.org)
2. Institute of Management Accountants (IMA) (www.imanet.org)
3. Association of Certified Fraud Examiners (ACFE) (www.acfe.com)
4. State CPA Societies (e.g., California Society of CPAs, New York State Society of CPAs)

Remember, the journey to becoming a successful accountant is a continuous process of learning, growth, and adaptation. Embrace these additional tips and resources to expand your knowledge, build a strong professional network, and stay ahead in the ever-evolving accounting landscape.

www.ingramcontent.com/pod-product-compliance
Lightning Source LLC
Chambersburg PA
CBHW071037240526
45469CB00006BD/2243